giving
nature
a home
rspb

This BLOOMSBURY Activity
Book belongs to:

BLOOMSBURY
Activity Books

On the busy riverbank

Add bird and insect stickers.

In the sunny garden

Add bird and insect stickers.

4

Feather fun

Colour in the bird feathers.

How to draw a robin

1. Draw two circles.

2. Add the wings and two lines.

3. Draw in the tail.

4. Add the feet, beak, and eyes.

Use this page to draw your robin.

The hungry blackbirds

Follow the lines and help the blackbirds get to the worms and rotten apples.

Nature patterns

Colour the animals to finish the patterns.

On a nature walk

Add butterfly, bee,
and bird stickers.

Colouring in fun

Pages 2-3

Pages 4-5

Pages 14–15

Pages 18–19

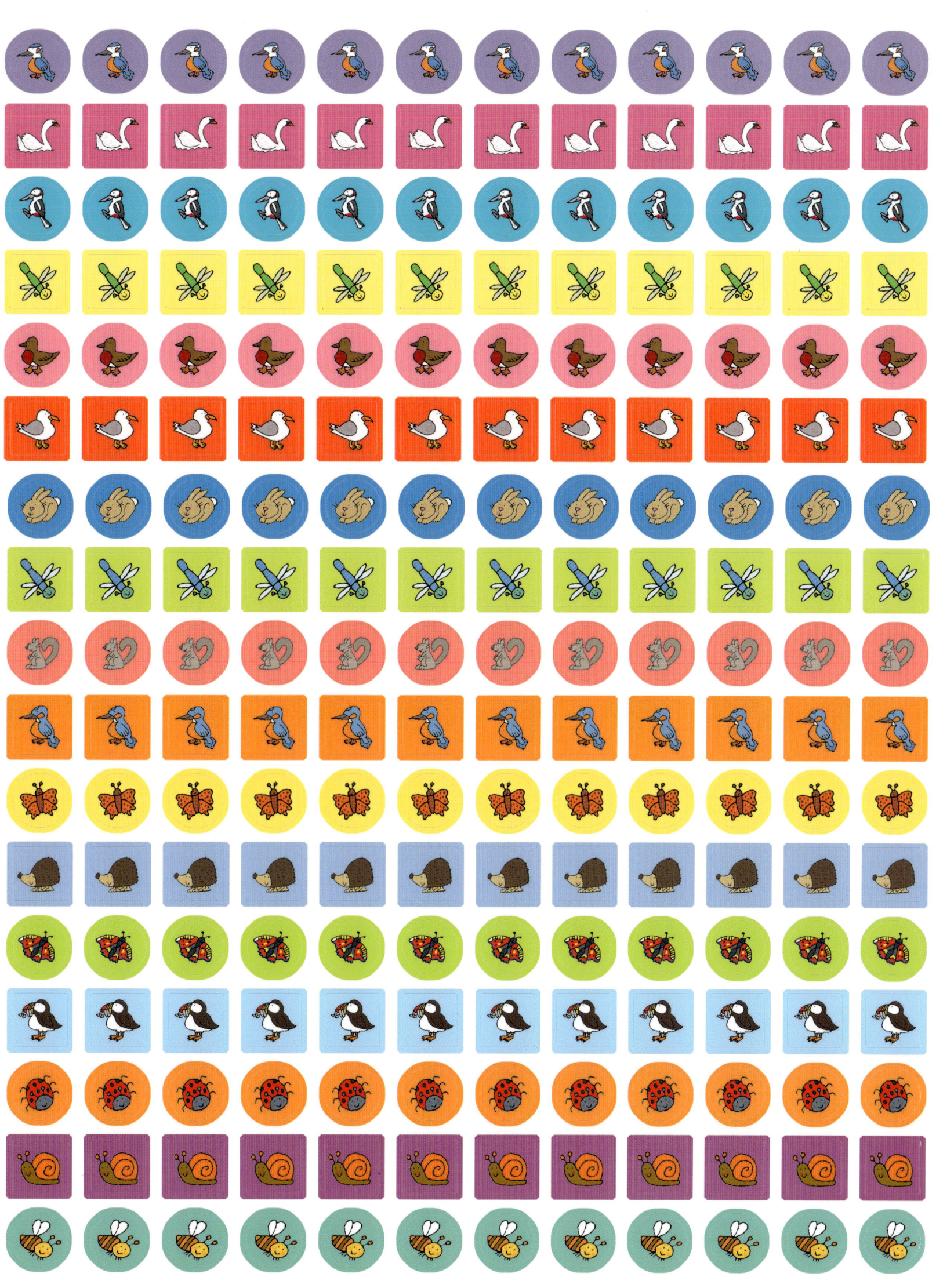

Colour the birds.

Feeding time

Make the two pictures the same by adding stickers to this page.

A bird jumble

Spot the odd one out in each group.

A walk in the park

Add bird, insect, and other animal stickers.

How to draw a fox

1. Draw three triangles.

2. Add the body.

3. Draw in the tail.

4. Add the face and tail tip.

Use this page to draw your fox.

The beach crowd

Add seabird stickers.

A nature puzzle

Help the hedgehog and toad through the maze to get to their friends.

My bird and nature spotter's guide

Keep a record here of any birds and other animals you see.

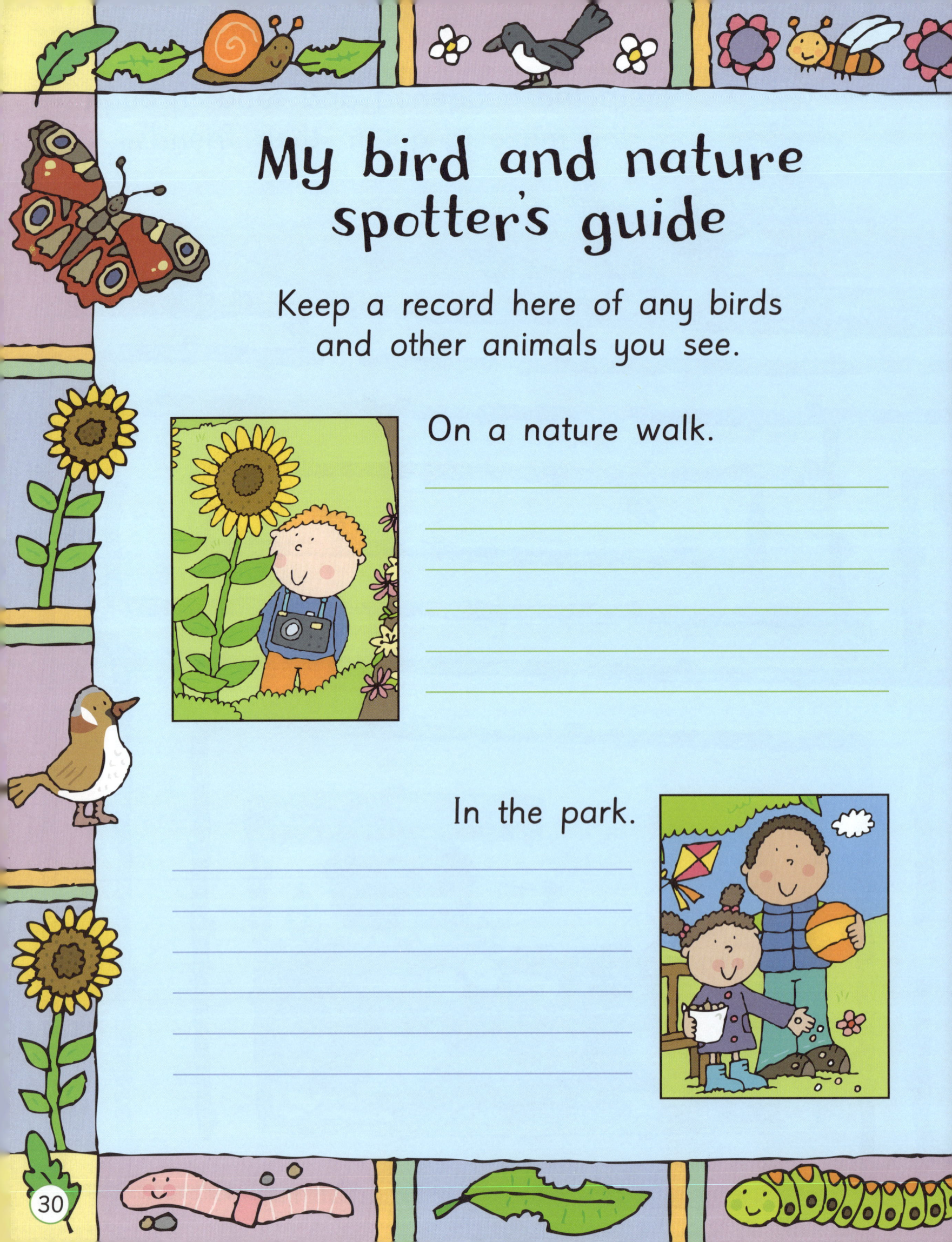

On a nature walk.

In the park.

At the seaside.

_____

_____

_____

_____

_____

_____

_____

_____

In the garden.

_____

_____

_____

_____

_____

_____

_____

31

Well done!

....

is a wildlife champion.

Date ....

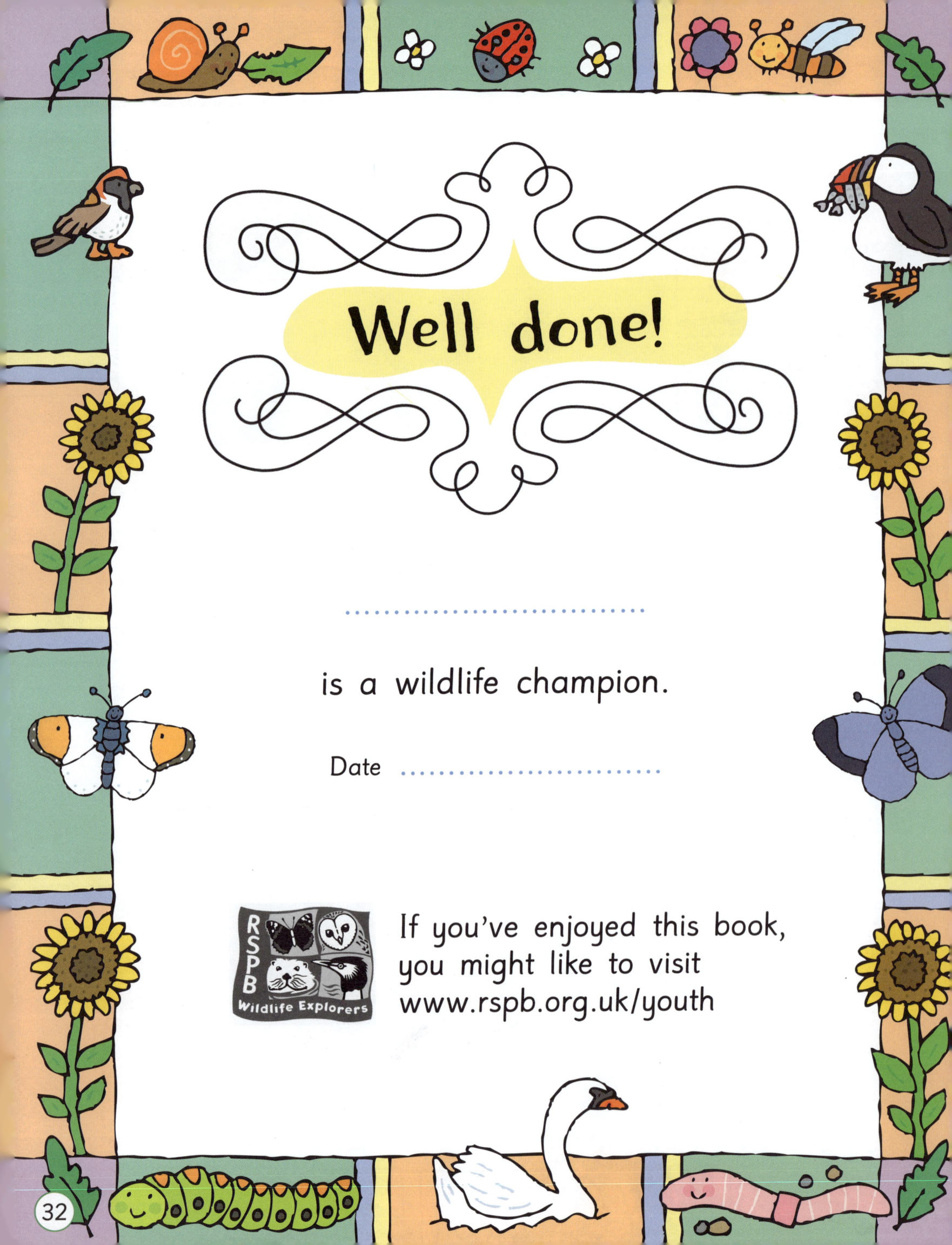

If you've enjoyed this book, you might like to visit www.rspb.org.uk/youth